All Scripture references taken from KJV unless otherwise indicated.

Courtroom Warfare @Midnight

Freshwater Press, 2023

Freshwaterpress9@gmail.com

ISBN: 978-1-960150-68-4

Table of Contents

The Psalms are used extensively in this warfare. It will be clear which Psalms are used for what as you read, but here they are for reference.

Commanding My Dreams

       Psalm 126, Psalm 136, Psalm 145, Psalm 16, Psalm 23, Psalm 40, Psalm 51

Triangular Powers,   Psalm 48

Defense Against Evil Petitions, Psalm 56, Psalm 66

Household Witchcraft: Psalm 55, Psalm 58, Ps 94

Every Evil Agent: Psalm 2, Psalm 18, Psalm 27, Psalm 35, Psalm 109

Where Is My Money?: Psalm 91

Extract Myself from Satan: Ps 92

Vengeance Belongs to God: Psalm 108

Courtroom Warfare
@ MIDNIGHT

Freshwater

At Midnight

It's MIDNIGHT, and we are going to BOLDLY to the Throne of God, to the Throne of Grace to receive Grace, Mercy and Help in time of trouble.

Lord JESUS, If I am none of yours, make me one of Yours, in the Name of Jesus. I believe that Jesus Christ is the Son of God and that He came to this Earth in flesh and gave up the Ghost on the Cross at Calvary, to redeem mankind back to the Father. And on the Third Day, God raised Him up again. I believe in the Resurrection of Jesus Christ.

HE LIVES! HE LIVES!

Lord, Jesus come into my heart and be the Lord of my life. Amen.

I believe by faith that I am in Covenant with You by the Better Blood of Jesus Christ, and *every other covenant with every other idol*, *little g god*, devil, demon, *familiar spirit*, *ancestral spirit*, and every other evil power of any idol that has required or demanded homage, sacrifice, and/or worship from me has ceased. And all other evil covenants are

broken by the power in the Blood of Jesus Christ. As well I plead the Blood of Jesus, and I am covered by the Blood of Jesus Christ.

Thank You Lord, I am a Protestant Christian who does **NOT** mix religions, traditions, cultures, superstitions, or foolishness; I abide by the Word of God only, in the Name of Jesus.

Thank You, Lord, because of my right relationship with You I can come at midnight, and I can ask for and receive the infilling of the Holy Spirit to overflowing. And I can come boldly to the Throne of Grace and Mercy, and plead my case right now, at midnight, in the Name of Jesus.

HOLY SPIRIT FIRE fall, in the Name of Jesus (X3)

Thank You, Lord, I am fearfully and wonderfully made.

And the Centurion told Jesus, *"Just speak the word and my servant will be healed."*

Speak the Word and we can all be healed, Lord. You sent His Word and healed them, You sent Your Word and healed us all--, all of mankind from sin-sickness. Thank You, Lord.

Now we are made *speaking spirits,* in the Name of Jesus. I can **speak,** and all things that obey You will obey Your Word as *I* speak. Spirits that must obey the Word of God, will hear the voice of the Word of God, and obey--, at midnight, and any time that it is spoken. Amen.

Thank You Lord, that even though if I *wish* a thing, or if I *think* a thing, and there is power in that, but Lord, I will **speak**, I must speak, to make Heaven and Earth agree. And I can have what I say because of the authority, and the dominion, and the power vested in me by the Better Covenant and by the Lord Jesus Christ, in the Name of Jesus. Amen.

Everything formed by God is perpetually subject to the Word--, that means me, you, all of Creation and even those things that would oppose any child of God. Lord, thank You for the authority the dominion, and the power, in the Name of Jesus.

LORD, hear my prayer, incline Your ear to my words, open up my heavens so that I may obtain Mercy and Grace before Your Throne, in the Name of Jesus.

Lord, open my spiritual eyes so I may see what is to be seen. So that I will know how to walk spiritually, so that I do not fall into any of the traps of the enemy, in the Name of Jesus. Amen.

Night Court

At MIDNIGHT, we are going boldly, we will go boldly to the Throne of Grace to obtain Mercy and Grace in the time of trouble, need.

I repent of all sins, I repent of evil doing, I repent of wickedness toward others; I repent of anything that would lock heavens over me, in the Name of Jesus. (Isaiah 59:1-2, Matthew 7:12).

Father, I repent of sin, transgression down my family line and ancestral line back even before Adam and Eve and ask You to Remove all bloodline and ancestral iniquity, by Your Mercy, in the Name of Jesus.

I retrieve my essence, in the Name of Jesus. Amen.

Father, break and remove any curses that I've caused to be created, as well as from my family line --from parents, their parents and even before them, in the Name of Jesus.

Father, if I am under Judgment from You, I appeal to your Mercy. Son of David, have MERCY upon me, (X3).

LORD, have Mercy on me. Lord, forgive me for all abominations I have committed against you:

incest, homosexuality, idol worship, foul alliances that I have made, among other sins, and the breaking any of the Ten Commandments, blasphemy, murder, abortion, stealing from God.

Thank You, Lord, that the prayers of the righteous availeth much power. Lord, I come to You at midnight, in prayer. Lord do not let me be powerless in the Spirit. Because of prayer, because of my prayers, Lord, I am no longer powerless in the Spirit. The prayers of the righteous availeth much power, Amen.

Hear my cry O Lord, incline Your ear to my prayers; from the ends of the Earth, I cry out to You.

In the whole armor of God and using the authority that you've given me to bind and *loose*:

I bind the *spirit of fear*. For You have not given us the *spirit of fear* but one of love, power and a sound mind. Amen.

Commanding My Dreams

As I prepare for bed, I establish how I will sleep tonight:

Dead people--, relatives or strangers, known or unknown, you will <u>not</u> appear in my dreams (X2, in the Name of Jesus.

Masquerades, I bind you from appearing in my dreams, in the Name of Jesus.

Lord, l ask that my dreams be from your Holy Spirit and not nightmares, night terrors, masquerades, trickery; Lord keep me from evil summons, keep me from going to realms where I should not go, in the sleep, in the dream, in the Name of Jesus.

If I am foolish, LORD, forgive me. **Help me**.

If I am ignorant, Lord, forgive me. Holy Spirit, **help me; teach me**. Give me a *teachable spirit*, in the Name of Jesus.

Lord, I ask for the *Spirits of Knowledge* and *Wisdom* so that I correctly apply knowledge in the Name of Jesus.

If I am captive, Lord, **help me**; do not leave my soul in hell. Send mighty Warrior Angels to disarm and bind the strongman jailers guarding me or *any* part of me that is captive and release me; do not leave my soul in hell, in the Name of Jesus.

If I am rebellious, Lord, **forgive me** and renew a right spirit in me. Because the wise man is prudent and follows the ways of the Lord, not being self-willed or following the ways that lead to hell, in the Name of Jesus.

Lord, let me be conscious and aware in the dream to express my Dominion as a child of God. I am a *speaking spirit*. Give me recall, Holy Spirit, in the dream to speak the Word of God to any entities, problems, situations, or issues that arise in the dream that are not of God. Amen.

Lord, if there have been dreams that You've given me that I do not/have not remembered, if my dreams have been *wiped*, I command that they be restored to me, in the Name of Jesus.

Backward Dreams

Let the invocation of my name, to summon me backward, die, in the Name of Jesus. Let the powers die.

Throne magic, throne witchcraft, throne wickedness, die, in the Name of Jesus.

Invisible bondages tying me down to the past, I break your chains, I break them, in the Name of Jesus.

Anti-progress powers in my dream, die, in the Name of Jesus.

Evil summons calling me backward to arrest my progress, die, in the Name of Jesus.

Consequences of all evil, backward dreams, be reversed by the Blood of Jesus, in the Name of Jesus.

All sacrifices against me be trumped by the power of the Blood of Jesus.

Satanic assignments by virtue of my blood, I reject you, in the Name of Jesus.

Dark covenants in my blood identifying me for darkness--, **Break! Break! Break!** by the Blood of Jesus, in the Name of Jesus.

Powers that have come for payment for what I did not buy, die by the Blood of Jesus, in Name of Jesus.

Whosoever is calling me backward and awaiting bad news from my life or my family, let your powers die, in the Name of Jesus.

Lord, remove **all** spiritual blinders from my eyes placed by the enemy, in Jesus' Name, Amen.

I bind *fear* and spiritual blindness so that I may see in the Spirit, in the Name of Jesus.

Lord, capture every evil assignment before it captures me, in the dream or in my awake life, in the Name of Jesus. (x3)

Lord, forgive me of sin, as it also brings spiritual dullness, ignorance, carnality, and blindness. Forgive me, Lord, I repent and ask forgiveness for every sin. Lord, I ask You to remove all iniquity, in the Name of Jesus.

Father do not allow my dreams to be *wiped* or forgotten, in the Name of Jesus.

Psalm 126 *(Commanding Dreams 1 of 7)*

When the LORD restored the fortunes of Zion,
we were like those who dream.

Then our mouth was filled with laughter,
and our tongue with shouts of joy;
then they said among the nations,

The LORD has done great things for them.
The LORD has done great things for us;
we are glad. (x2)

Restore our fortunes, O LORD,
like streams in the Negeb!

Those who sow in tears shall reap with shouts of
joy!
He who goes out weeping,
bearing the seed for sowing,
shall come home with shouts of joy,
bringing his sheaves with him. ESV
In the Name of Jesus.

Psalm 136 *(Commanding Dreams 2 of 7)*

Oh, give thanks to the L<small>ORD</small>, for *He is* good!
For His mercy *endures* forever.

Oh, give thanks to the God of gods!
For His mercy *endures* forever.

Oh, give thanks to the Lord of lords!
For His mercy *endures* forever:

To Him who alone does great wonders,
For His mercy *endures* forever;

To Him who by wisdom made the heavens,
For His mercy *endures* forever;

To Him who laid out the earth above the waters,
For His mercy *endures* forever;

To Him who made great lights,
For His mercy *endures* forever—

The sun to rule by day,
For His mercy *endures* forever;

The moon and stars to rule by night,
For His mercy *endures* forever.

To Him who struck Egypt in their firstborn,
For His mercy *endures* forever;

And brought out Israel from among them,
For His mercy *endures* forever;

With a strong hand, and with an outstretched
arm,
For His mercy *endures* forever;

To Him who divided the Red Sea in two,
For His mercy *endures* forever;

And made Israel pass through the midst of it,
For His mercy *endures* forever;

But overthrew Pharaoh and his army in the Red
Sea,
For His mercy *endures* forever;

To Him who led His people through the
wilderness,
For His mercy *endures* forever;

To Him who struck down great kings,
For His mercy *endures* forever;

And slew famous kings,
For His mercy *endures* forever—

Sihon king of the Amorites,
For His mercy *endures* forever;

And Og king of Bashan,
For His mercy *endures* forever—

And gave their land as a heritage,
For His mercy *endures* forever;

A heritage to Israel His servant,
For His mercy *endures* forever.

Who remembered us in our lowly state,
For His mercy *endures* forever;

And rescued us from our enemies,
For His mercy *endures* forever;

Who gives food to all flesh,
For His mercy *endures* forever.

Oh, give thanks to the God of heaven!
For His mercy *endures* forever.

Psalm 145 *(Commanding Dreams 3 of 7)*

I will extol You, my God, O King;
And I will bless Your name forever and ever.

Every day I will bless You,
And I will praise Your name forever and ever.

Great *is* the LORD, and greatly to be praised;
And His greatness *is* unsearchable.

One generation shall praise Your works to another,
And shall declare Your mighty acts.

I will meditate on the glorious splendor of Your majesty,

And on Your wondrous works.

Men shall speak of the might of Your awesome acts,
And I will declare Your greatness.

They shall utter the memory of Your great goodness,
And shall sing of Your righteousness.

The LORD *is* gracious and full of compassion,
Slow to anger and great in mercy.

The LORD *is* good to all,
And His tender mercies *are* over all His works.

All Your works shall praise You, O LORD,
And Your saints shall bless You.

They shall speak of the glory of Your kingdom,
And talk of Your power,

To make known to the sons of men His mighty
acts,
And the glorious majesty of His kingdom.

Your kingdom *is* an everlasting kingdom,
And Your dominion *endures* throughout
all generations.

The LORD upholds all who fall,
And raises up all *who are* bowed down.

The eyes of all look expectantly to You,
And You give them their food in due season.

You open Your hand
And satisfy the desire of every living thing.

The LORD *is* righteous in all His ways,
Gracious in all His works.

The LORD *is* near to all who call upon Him,
To all who call upon Him in truth.

He will fulfill the desire of those who fear Him;
He also will hear their cry and save them.

The LORD preserves all who love Him,
But all the wicked He will destroy.

My mouth shall speak the praise of the LORD,
And all flesh shall bless His holy name
Forever and ever. Amen.

Lord, restore my dream life in the Name of Jesus.
It is the intoxicated, inebriated, captive, deceived
and tricked people who have *wiped* dreams.
LORD do not let me be in that category, or in that
ilk, in the Name of Jesus.

Preserve me, O God, for in You I put my trust.

O my soul, you have said to the LORD,
"You *are* my Lord,
My goodness is nothing apart from You."

As for the saints who *are* on the earth,
"They are the excellent ones, in whom is all my
delight."

Their sorrows shall be multiplied who
hasten *after* another *god;*
Their drink offerings of blood I will not offer,
Nor take up their names on my lips.

O LORD, *You are* the portion of my inheritance
and my cup;
You maintain my lot.

The lines have fallen to me in pleasant *places;*
Yes, I have a good inheritance.

I will bless the LORD who has given me counsel;
My heart also instructs me in the night seasons.

I have set the LORD always before me;
Because *He is* at my right hand I shall not be
moved.

Therefore my heart is glad, and my glory rejoices;
My flesh also will rest in hope.

For You will not leave my soul in Sheol,
Nor will You allow Your Holy One to see corruption.

You will show me the path of life;
In Your presence *is* fullness of joy;
At Your right hand *are* pleasures forevermore.

Thank You, Lord, Amen.

The LORD *is* my shepherd;
I shall not want.

He makes me to lie down in green pastures;
He leads me beside the still waters.

He restores my soul;
He leads me in the paths of righteousness
For His name's sake.

Yea, though I walk through the valley of the
shadow of death,
I will fear no evil;
For You *are* with me;
Your rod and Your staff, they comfort me.

You prepare a table before me in the presence of
my enemies;
You anoint my head with oil;
My cup runs over.

Surely goodness and mercy shall follow me
All the days of my life;
And I will dwell in the house of the LORD
Forever. **AMEN**

Psalm 40 *(Commanding Dreams 6 of 5)*

I waited patiently for the LORD;
And He inclined to me,
And heard my cry.

He also brought me up out of a horrible pit,
Out of the miry clay,
And set my feet upon a rock,
And established my steps.

He has put a new song in my mouth—
Praise to our God;
Many will see *it* and fear,
And will trust in the LORD.

Blessed *is* that man who makes the LORD his
trust,
And does not respect the proud, nor such as turn
aside to lies.

Many, O LORD my God, *are* Your wonderful
works
Which You have done;
And Your thoughts toward us
Cannot be recounted to You in order;
If I would declare and speak *of them,*
They are more than can be numbered.
Sacrifice and offering You did not desire;
My ears You have opened.
Burnt offering and sin offering You did not

require.

Then I said, "Behold, I come;
In the scroll of the book *it is* written of me.

I delight to do Your will, O my God,
And Your law *is* within my heart."

I have proclaimed the good news of
righteousness
In the great assembly;
Indeed, I do not restrain my lips,
O LORD, You Yourself know.

I have not hidden Your righteousness within my
heart;
I have declared Your faithfulness and Your
salvation;
I have not concealed Your lovingkindness and
Your truth
From the great assembly.

Do not withhold Your tender mercies from me,
O LORD;
Let Your lovingkindness and Your truth
continually preserve me.

For innumerable evils have surrounded me;
My iniquities have overtaken me, so that I am not
able to look up;
They are more than the hairs of my head;
Therefore my heart fails me.

Be pleased, O LORD, to deliver me;
O LORD, make haste to help me!

Let them be ashamed and brought to mutual
confusion
Who seek to destroy my life;
Let them be driven backward and brought to
dishonor
Who wish me evil.

Let them be confounded because of their shame,
Who say to me, "Aha, aha!"

Let all those who seek You rejoice and be glad in
You;
Let such as love Your salvation say continually,
"The LORD be magnified!"

But I *am* poor and needy;
Yet the LORD thinks upon me.
You *are* my help and my deliverer;
Do not delay, O my God.

AMEN.

Psalm 51 *(Commanding Dreams 7 of 7)*

Have mercy upon me, O God,
According to Your lovingkindness;
According to the multitude of Your tender
mercies,
Blot out my transgressions.

Wash me thoroughly from my iniquity,
And cleanse me from my sin.

For I acknowledge my transgressions,
And my sin *is* always before me.

Against You, You only, have I sinned,
And done *this* evil in Your sight—
That You may be found just when You speak,
And blameless when You judge.

Behold, I was brought forth in iniquity,
And in sin my mother conceived me.

Behold, You desire truth in the inward parts,
And in the hidden *part* You will make me to
know wisdom.
Purge me with hyssop, and I shall be clean;
Wash me, and I shall be whiter than snow.

Make me hear joy and gladness,
That the bones You have broken may rejoice.

Hide Your face from my sins,
And blot out all my iniquities.

Create in me a clean heart, O God,
And renew a steadfast spirit within me.

Do not cast me away from Your presence,
And do not take Your Holy Spirit from me.

Restore to me the joy of Your salvation,
And uphold me *by Your* generous Spirit.

Then I will teach transgressors Your ways,
And sinners shall be converted to You.

Deliver me from the guilt of bloodshed, O God,
The God of my salvation,
And my tongue shall sing aloud of Your
righteousness.

O Lord, open my lips,
And my mouth shall show forth Your praise.

For You do not desire sacrifice, or else I would
give *it;*
You do not delight in burnt offering.

The sacrifices of God *are* a broken spirit,
A broken and a contrite heart—
These, O God, You will not despise.

Do good in Your good pleasure to Zion;
Build the walls of Jerusalem.

Then You shall be pleased with the sacrifices of
righteousness,
With burnt offering and whole burnt offering;
Then they shall offer bulls on Your altar.

Cancel All Initiations

At midnight Lord, I come to You. I come to cancel all evil initiations! I Cancel every evil initiation.

Lord, in the Name of Jesus, I cancel every evil initiation – known, unknown, juvenile, childish, adult, by trickery, foolishness, tradition, culture, entrapment, in the waking life or in the dream life, hidden or right in plain view, in my face, in Jesus' Name.

I reverse every evil word I have spoken where I have repeated others, or repeated words or word curses over myself. I break every evil oath, ever evil vow, every evil word curse, I break them, and I reverse their effects over my life now, in the Name of Jesus.

Lord, redeem me, rescue me from every evil kingdom, any ungodly kingdoms or lockup, any ungodly place where I should never have been--, any occultic place, witchcraft place, animalistic--. Anything that has taken me from grace to grass – anything that has taken me, or any part of me. Any kingdom where I have found an idol and worshipped it, even for one second, one part of a second, Lord, forgive me, in the Name of Jesus.

Lord, I am sorry for my ignorance, my rebellion, my stupidity, my naivete. I renounce all evil covenants made, in the Name of Jesus.

Bind Up Fear

I bind up the *spirit of fear*.

As long as I am doing what God has instructed me, I fear nothing, I fear no man or what man can do for me. I do not fear the criticism or the judgment. I do not have a need for any man's approval, in the Name of Jesus.

Lord, I bless You; I bind *fear* and I bless You. You have comforted me on all sides; you have left us The Comforter for this life, thank You LORD. You have satisfied my mouth with good things, in the Name of Jesus.

Lord, I refuse fear, I reject and eject fear from my life, because You have not given me the *spirit of fear*, but of power and of love and of a sound mind. ***I bind the spirit of fear,*** in the Name of Jesus, I cast it out of my life, in the Name of Jesus.

Every power behind every activity of *fear* in my life, receive the wrath of God and be consumed in it, in the Name of Jesus.

By the power of the Lord Jesus Christ nothing that I fear or have ever been afraid of will come upon me, in the Name of Jesus. Amen.

Lord, no family evils, harm, hurts, disasters or disappointments shall come upon me, in the Name of Jesus. Amen

Lord, let nothing that I **see, hear, smell, feel or sense** in the dream, or in the Spirit cause me fear or consternation. The Lord is with me and nothing can ever separate me from Him or take me out of His hands and His care, in the Name of Jesus. The Lord is with me and nothing can ever separate me from Him (X2), in the Name of Jesus.

I wear the whole armor of God, the helmet of salvation, the breastplate of righteousness, the shield of faith, my loins are gird about with truth, my feet are shod with the preparation of the Gospel of Peace. I wear the cloak of zeal and garments of vengeance by the Lord, in the Name of Jesus, and I watch and pray, in the Name of Jesus.

His rod and staff, they comfort me. The Name of the LORD is a strong tower the righteous run into it and they are safe.

In Christ, with Christ, nothing by any means can hurt me. At the Name of Jesus every knee must bow of things in the earth in the heavens, in the sea, even beneath the earth and beneath the seas, in every realm, in the Name of Jesus.

The Lord is a Man of War: the Lord is His name. Jehovah Sabaoth, Mighty God. Mighty God. Mighty God.

In Him I am more than a conqueror, Amen.

Backsliding shall not be my portion in the Name of Jesus.

I bind and cast out *fear* of losing my anointing and salvation in the Name of Jesus.

I bind and cast out every *fear* of compromising my faith, in the Name of Jesus.

I bind and cast out the *fear* of being tempted beyond resistance; Holy Spirit strengthen me, strengthen my resolve and my resistance to evil and sin, in the Name of Jesus.

I break every evil covenant that has brought *fear* into my life, in the Name of Jesus.

I command every night terror that has brought fear into my world to **stop, stop, stop,** and move far away from me, in the Name of Jesus.

You, *spirit of fear*, lose your hold upon my life and my family, in the Name of Jesus.

I command all evil human agents using the *spirit of fear* in all of its manifestations to cease and desist. Cease and desist. Cease and desist, in the Name of Jesus. By the power of God, you shall not and no longer terrify me in the night, in the dream, in the sleep or even in my awake hours. I command you to stumble, fall, and never get up again, in the Name of Jesus.

The fear and terror of unbelievers is not my lot, in the Name of Jesus. My tomorrow is blessed by Christ Jesus, Amen. My tomorrow is blessed by Christ Jesus, Amen.

My destiny is attached to God; therefore, I decree that I cannot fail, God is the greatest power, in the Name of Jesus. God is the greatest power. God is the Greatest Power, in the Name of Jesus (X3).

Every bondage and its yoke, because of *the spirit of fear*, I break you, I disorganize you, I dismantle you, in the Name of Jesus.

Any and every evil door the *spirit of fear* has opened in my life or opened, for you to do any damage to me, I now close it all; I close it and I seal it, now in the Name of Jesus.

Every disease, oppression, depression as a result of *fear*, disappear now, in the Name of Jesus.

Nightmares, night terrors, I reject you, I refuse you, I send you to a big spiritual dumpster and set that dumpster on FIRE ignited by the Thunder and Lightning of God, BURN! BURN! BURN! Amen.

I nullify every writing, contract, agreement, covenant against my work, my profession, and career, and burn it all to ashes, in the Name of Jesus.

Lord, You delight in the prosperity of Your people, bless me, indeed in my career, profession and work, in the Name of Jesus.

Every enchantment, invocation and ritual of *fear* being made against me, I neutralize you and command you to fail against me, in the Name of Jesus.

Every gathering of enemies in any location against me, shall not stand, in the Name of Jesus.

All evil arrangements of the devil concerning my life, my home, my marriage, my spouse, my children, my family, my career, my ministry, my health, my purpose and destiny—you shall not stand, nor come to pass, in the Name of Jesus.

I destroy all efforts of the enemy to frustrate my work, my marriage, my children, my spouse, my life, in the Name of Jesus.

Lord, let all those who are against me without a cause in my place of work turn back and be brought to confusion and shame, in the Name of Jesus.

Lord, let those who have gathered against me even *with* a cause, Blood of Jesus cry me out of every trouble, in the Name of Jesus.

I close every door that the enemy has used to gain access to any part of my life – work, education, career, marriage, family--, my life is hid in Christ, therefore the enemy cannot kill me. The enemy cannot kill any part of my life. Anyone trying--, back to sender, I send your enchantments, your arrows, your curses back to sender! Go back, kill yourself, in the Name of Jesus.

I seal those doors with the Holy Spirit of Promise, in the Name of Jesus.

Let every territorial *spirit* working against us in our neighborhood be frustrated, bound and cast out, in the Name of Jesus.

Let every power contrary to the power of God operating to suppress people in my area be neutralized, in the Name of Jesus.

I bind every *spirit of frustration, defeat, delayed blessings, backwardness,* and *fear* in my environment, in the Name of Jesus.

I banish every enemy of progress in my neighborhood, and in my life, in the Name of Jesus.

I bind the *spirits of death, armed robbery* and *assassination* in my neighborhood, in the Name of Jesus.

I reject, renounce and destroy every evil agreement or covenant in the environment, in the Name of Jesus.

By the Blood of Jesus, I nullify the effects and operation of evil forces in, near, or around my house, in the Name of Jesus.

Lord, get all my stubborn pursuers occupied with unprofitable assignments so they don't bother me, in the Name of Jesus.

By the Blood of Jesus I nullify the effects and operation of evil forces around my workplace, or by my school or my children's schools, in the Name of Jesus.

In Jesus mighty name, I fire back every arrow, every spiritual bullet and satanic missile fired at me. Lord, reveal the secrets and expose all my enemies masquerading as *friends*, in the Name of Jesus.

Father, Lord, make it impossible for my enemies to use my foot marks, urine, feces, hair, clothing, shoes, nails, pads, pictures-- anything to do with me, against me, my children or family, in the Name of Jesus. Amen.

I command you, *monitoring spirits* get out, get out of my life, get out of my house, in the Name of Jesus. Take every gadget, device and monitoring technology you have with you, in the Name of Jesus.

I command you, *familiar spirits* and ancestral strongmen, GET OUT! get out of my house, get out of my life, in the Name of Jesus.

I command you, *servient spirits*, GET OUT! in the Name of Jesus. I command you out of me, out of my life, out of my children, out of my house, out of my business, career, and education, in the Name of Jesus.

Lord, I repent of all generational sin and ask You to remove all iniquity from my family line by Your Mercy, and Your Grace and by Your loving kindness toward us all, in the Name of Jesus.

Father, in every way my **mind** is connecting me to the life that my forefather's lived--, if it is blessing to me and my life, I receive it in the Name of Jesus. If it is a curse to me and my life, I command my mind to come under the authority of the Word and the Spirit of God. I cast down every evil imagination that exalts itself against the knowledge of God, in Jesus' Name.

Let this mind be in me that was also in Christ Jesus, Amen. (Eccl 1:8-11, Isaiah 40:22)

Lord, the words I speak are Spirit and they are life. Spirit doesn't die – Lord let every word I speak, speak life. Let every word I speak, speak life to the good things in life, the things of God. Let the meditation of my heart and the words I speak, be acceptable to You, my God, my Redeemer. Let all the words I speak and the thoughts in my mind bring life, bring peace, bring goodness and abundance, to my life and to my bloodline, to the Glory of God, in the Name of Jesus.

The Word of God can give life, it can kill, it can translate – Lord, You entrust me with Your Word, with the power of Your Word.

So with your Word, just like You, I rout out, I pluck up, I pull down, all the works and efforts of the enemy, in the Name of Jesus.

I build up, and rebuild all the works of Your hands, all the good things planned and designed for my life and the life of my bloodline, in the Name of Jesus.

I cast down every imagination and every high thing that exalts itself against the knowledge of God.

I cast down foolish thoughts that the devil presents, either directly, through people, through TV, media, social media, doomsday scrolling, visions or situations in my life, in the Name of Jesus.

I reject and rebuke all twisted words that the devil has employed against me. I forbid the enemy to twist my words against me. All twisting and tormenting words of the devil, I rebuke you, I reject you, I eject you from my life. I bind you from speaking to me in the Name of Jesus.

I repent of and renounce ever singing words of unbelief, disbelief, destruction, terror, lies, all works of the flesh because it played on the radio, TV, movie or other device and it was popular or sounded cool or good, in the Name of Jesus. Lord, forgive me.

Lord, I ask that you cover all those evil words, lyrics and phrases that I have spoken, chanted, sung, or rapped with the Blood of Jesus and let them not come to fruition in my life, in the Name of Jesus. Amen.

Lord, let the Words I speak, and the meditation of my heart be acceptable to You, O Lord, my Redeemer.

Lord, thank You for dreams to see the things I cannot see in the natural, that I cannot yet see--, flashbacks and parenthetical, prophetic visions, in the Name of Jesus. Thank You for those.

Dreams and visions to see--, both to see and understand—and not be afraid of what I see, and not be afraid to understand, thank You, Lord.

Lord, make me aware in the dream. Do not let me be tricked, deceived, or duped.

Lord, forgive me for being ignorant. Keep me from being ignorant as ignorance is the same plane as evil *spirits* and that is where they have access to me, in the Name of Jesus.

Lord, let me be conscious and not clueless in the dream state. Lord, give me dream state awareness, give me spiritual awareness, in the Name of Jesus. And, Lord, give me knowledge with Wisdom to know what to do with the knowledge that I'm given.

I must remember what I do in the Spirit, what I do in the dream, in the Name of Jesus.

Lord, I break all demonic soul ties with evil idols, and entities, powers, wickedness, celestial beings, in the Name of Jesus.

Break all soul ties with any type of *spirit spouse*.

Lord, if my life, health, money, marital destiny has been used as a sacrifice, I cancel that sacrifice now, in the Name of Jesus.

Anything keeping me from being pregnant in the natural – I break all soul ties with all evil entities in the spiritual world, now, in the Name of Jesus.

I abort every spiritual pregnancy of any type formed knowingly, unknowingly, by stupidity, ignorance, or rebellion, in the Name of Jesus.

Lord, thank You for showing me signs in my dreams to know if I am soul tied or connected or married in the spirit to incubus or succubus, in the Name of Jesus.

Lord, thank You for proper dream interpretation, because what seems good may not be good, what seems bad, may not be bad. Lord, You know. Help me to know, in the Name of Jesus.

Triangular Powers: Sun, Moon, Stars

Lord, I'm up **at midnight** to make these decrees and declarations. And I am speaking also because of my star, in the Name of Jesus.

Sun, do not smite me by day.

Moon and stars, do not smite me by night or at any time. I reprogram you so that no evil comes upon me during your watch in the Name of Jesus.

Earth and all celestial elements, hear the Word of the Lord -- you were created to declare the glory of God. You shall work in my favor, never against me. God is glorified in my health, peace, prosperity, and in my abundance, in the Name of Jesus.

Earth, O Earth if you are visiting records and judgments of misconduct from my forefathers, my ancestors, Earth do not testify against me, in the Name of Jesus.

Do not use the mistakes of my past against me, in the night hours, or ever, in the Name of Jesus.

Testify instead, against the enemies of God, do not testify against me, in the Name of Jesus.

I am here at midnight, and I am talking to the stars, Lord.

Psalm 48 *(Triangular Powers 1of 1)*

Great *is* the LORD, and greatly to be praised
In the city of our God, *In* His holy mountain.

Beautiful in elevation, The joy of the whole
earth, *is* Mount Zion *on* the sides of the north,
The city of the great King.

God *is* in her palaces; He is known as her refuge.

For behold, the kings assembled,
They passed by together.

They saw *it, and* so they marveled;
They were troubled, they hastened away.

Fear took hold of them there,
And pain, as of a woman in birth pangs,

As when You break the ships of Tarshish
With an east wind.

As we have heard,
So we have seen
In the city of the LORD of hosts,
In the city of our God:
God will establish it forever. *Selah*
We have thought, O God, on Your
lovingkindness,

In the midst of Your temple.

According to Your name, O God,
So *is* Your praise to the ends of the earth;
Your right hand is full of righteousness.

Let Mount Zion rejoice,
Let the daughters of Judah be glad,
Because of Your judgments.

Walk about Zion,
And go all around her.
Count her towers;

Mark well her bulwarks;
Consider her palaces;
That you may tell *it* to the generation following.

For this *is* God,
Our God forever and ever;
He will be our guide
Even to death.
AMEN.

Stars, O Stars: Pleaides, Orion, Mazzaroth, Arcturus, I break every covenant, contract, agreement, certificate, oath, and vow entangling me with Pleaides, Orion, Mazzoroth (Job 38:32), and Arcturus, including all related books of wisdom, books of knowledge, books of philosophy, books of time travel, Freemasonic books, and all other evil sacred books and command that they be stamped with the Blood of Jesus. I call for them to be nailed to the Cross of Jesus Christ and burned with holy consuming fire.

 I declare that you have no further authority over me to enact evil against me in the Name of Jesus.

Anyone one invoking your powers against me, have their curses, spells and enchantments go back to them 7-fold in the Name of Jesus.

In the Name of Jesus, I lift up a standard against any power working against me in the heavenlies, against every evil projection from every evil altar, I come and I raise a standard. (Isaiah 54:17 and Isaiah 59:19).

Cancel All Death Judgements

Lord, I pray for Mercy, in the Name of Jesus.

I cancel all death judgements against me in the Name of Jesus. (Isaiah 28:18)

Any treaty I have made with death will be abolished and any agreement I have made with the grave or with hell be broken in the Name of Jesus. It shall be cancelled, thank You, Lord.

Any agreement with death to my body, marriage, finances – Heavenly Father we ask Your Mercy and divine intervention to destroy any covenant of Death, grave or hell that is attacking me, family or life, by the Blood of Jesus. I break every evil covenant linked with death, the grave and hell in Jesus' Name.

Every evil altar of death, the grave, and hell erected against me, be dismantled and destroyed by Fire, in Jesus' Name.

I command all evil powers who want to retaliate or arrest me because of this prayer, be arrested by the Fire of the Holy Ghost, in the Name of Jesus.

Negative prophecies of sudden death, accidents and incidents against me and my family, and my life, be canceled in Jesus' Name.

I command all *spirits of death* in all areas of my life to come OUT! Come out, come out, in Jesus' Name.

All *death spirits*, I curse you and bind you, and destroy you, in Jesus' Name.

I command health, life and healing to me, to myself, my life, my family, in the Name of Jesus.

I shall not die, but I shall live and declare the works of the Lord in the land of the living, amen!

Carnality is caused by a lack of knowledge; Lord, do not let carnality entrap me, LORD, don't let me be ignorant, in the Name of Jesus.

Lord, release warrior angels, morning stars, archangels, thrones, dominions, governors, cherubim, seraphim--, to rescue me from all captivity and all evil planned against me, whichever angels must come, release them, Lord, send them, in the Name of Jesus.

Give me the presence of mind, the presence of Your Angels, so that nothing by any means can harm me. Give me the presence of those Angels so I will not be harmed, in the Name of Jesus.

Christ in me--, the hope of Glory. God in your name, the forces of evil shall bow. They shall hear my voice and listen when I speak. Resurrection power, quicken this mortal body, in the Name of Jesus.

Presence of GOD burn and burn brightly to scare off every evil demon, every devil, every evil human persecutor, every evil human perpetrator, in the Name of Jesus.

My life, receive Fire, become Fire
(X3).

BURN BURN BURN, every brightly – burn them, burn them, burn them up in the Name of Jesus. Every evil doer, be consumed by the unapproachable Light of God. Go into oblivion. Go! Go into oblivion. Disappear, forever in the Name of Jesus.

Dead relatives, dead friends, masquerades get out of my life forever in the Name of Jesus.

Powers of the grave, release my finances now, in the Name of Jesus. (X3)

Powers of the grave release my business now, in the Name of Jesus. (X3)

Powers of hell, death and the grave, release my life and every part of my family's life in the Name of Jesus.

Release it! Release it! Release it, now, in the Name of Jesus.

Lord, by your Power, I take dominion in the spiritual realm – Lord, give me the presence of mind to say, Jesus! The Blood of Jesus. The Blood of Jesus. The Blood of Jesus is against you, in the Name of Jesus.

I command the Flaming Sword of the Lord, the Razor of the Lord and the Fiery Sword of God to cut you into irreplaceable pieces to all interlopers in my dream life, and in my life in any way, in the Name of Jesus.

Lord, any creature (*spirit, entity*) that I meet in the dream, let me conquer them, completely, without fear, without trepidation, because You O Lord, are with me, and I am in You, in the Name of Jesus.

FIRE of GOD, consume them completely, in the Name of Jesus.

Any evil judgments of death from evil courts against me, I shoot you down with the Word of God and the Fire of the Holy Ghost, in the Name of Jesus (X2) (Isaiah 28:18).

Any evil verdicts of death from evil courts against me, I shoot you down with the Word of God and the Fire of the Holy Ghost, in the Name of Jesus.

Any evil verdict of death from **any** court against me, I shoot you down with the Word of God, and the Fire of the Holy Ghost.

Lord, whatever entity or evil I meet in any dream, in the spirit, in the night, I conquer them, I conquer them, through Christ Jesus, because through Christ, I am more than a conqueror, Amen.

Shadows, shadow people, caskets – by the power in the Blood of Jesus, I reverse your evil verdict against me, in the Name of Jesus. I release your judgment against me, in the Name of Jesus. I reverse your judgment against me, in the Name of Jesus. I reject your judgement against me in the Name of Jesus. You die, not me. You die, in the Name of Jesus, not me. You die, in Jesus' Name.

Shadows, monitoring spirits, shadow people, caskets, all evil powers, you die, in the Name of Jesus. (Isaiah 28:18)

Break Covenant with A Deity

I plead the Blood of Jesus. I am in Christ, and I bear in my body the marks of the Lord Jesus Christ.

I bind the strongman that is pursuing me to try to enforce the curse, in the Name of Jesus.

Devil, I remove your altar in my life, from my body – anywhere idols are in me, near me, in my heart. I replace you completely with the Highest Altar—the Most High God, that of the Lord Jesus Christ – that of the Better Covenant forged by the Better Blood. Amen.

I break every evil covenant with the devil and any and every one of his representatives. And I further bind them from emanating any evil against me, any curses, yokes, bondages, death, destruction into my life and the life of my family and bloodline, in the Name of Jesus.

Father, in the Name of Jesus, I come against every evil petition that has been raised against me or my family members in any age, era, realm, timeline or dimension, past present or future to infinity in the Name of Jesus. I come against every evil petition that has been raised against me or any of my family members, in any spiritual Court in Jesus' Name.

I follow peace with all men. I do not go popping off of on anyone. I agree with my adversary quickly, in the natural, in the Name of Jesus.

Anyone, any entity filing a petition against me in the Spirit at the Throne of Grace, or in the Court of Zion, the Court of Mediation, the Court of the Petition, in the Court of Watchers, in Court of Witnesses--, Lord, by revealing to me that this is happening by revealing it in my dreams and proper, correct, Christian dream interpretation— for every dream where You have shown me a throne, or evil people around a throne, I know there are evil petitions against me, before the Lord.

And I reverse all evil verdicts, edicts, all evil judgments against me, in the Name of Jesus, by the power in the Blood of Jesus.

For every time You've shown me someone chasing me with a weapon, Lord I come to the Courts of the Lord to defend myself against evil petitions that are **secretly** being presented against me to get death sentences against me—to steal, kill or destroy me or anything about me or anything under my stewardship. I present myself and my case in the Courts at the Throne(s) of the Lord, in the Name of Jesus. Amen.

Defense Against Evil Petitions

Psalm 56 *(1of 2)*

Be merciful to me, O God, for man would
swallow me up;
Fighting all day he oppresses me.

My enemies would hound *me* all day,
For *there are* many who fight against me, O
Most High.
Whenever I am afraid,
I will trust in You.

In God (I will praise His word),
In God I have put my trust;
I will not fear.
What can flesh do to me?

All day they twist my words;
All their thoughts *are* against me for evil.

They gather together,
They hide, they mark my steps,

When they lie in wait for my life.

Shall they escape by iniquity?
In anger cast down the peoples, O God!

You number my wanderings;
Put my tears into Your bottle;
Are they not in Your book?

When I cry out *to You,*
Then my enemies will turn back;
This I know, because God *is* for me.

In God (I will praise *His* word),
In the LORD (I will praise *His* word),

In God I have put my trust;
I will not be afraid.
What can man do to me?

Vows *made* to You *are binding* upon me, O God;
I will render praises to You,

For You have delivered my soul from death.
Have You not *kept* my feet from falling,
That I may walk before God
In the light of the living?
Amen.

Defense Against Evil Petitions

Psalm 66 *(2 of 2)*

Make a joyful shout to God, all the earth!

Sing out the honor of His name;
Make His praise glorious.

Say to God,
"How awesome are Your works!
Through the greatness of Your power
Your enemies shall submit themselves to You.

All the earth shall worship You
And sing praises to You;
They shall sing praises *to* Your name." *Selah*
Come and see the works of God;
He is awesome *in His* doing toward the sons of
men.

He turned the sea into dry *land;*
They went through the river on foot.
There we will rejoice in Him.

He rules by His power forever;
His eyes observe the nations;
Do not let the rebellious exalt themselves. *Selah*
Oh, bless our God, you peoples!
And make the voice of His praise to be heard,

Who keeps our soul among the living,
And does not allow our feet to be moved.

For You, O God, have tested us;
You have refined us as silver is refined.

You brought us into the net;
You laid affliction on our backs.

You have caused men to ride over our heads;
We went through fire and through water;
But You brought us out to rich *fulfillment.*

I will go into Your house with burnt offerings; I
will pay You my vows,

Which my lips have uttered
And my mouth has spoken when I was in trouble.

I will offer You burnt sacrifices of fat animals,
With the sweet aroma of rams;
I will offer bulls with goats. *Selah*

Come *and* hear, all you who fear God,
And I will declare what He has done for my soul.

I cried to Him with my mouth,
And He was extolled with my tongue.

If I regard iniquity in my heart,
The Lord will not hear.

But certainly God has heard *me;*
He has attended to the voice of my prayer.

Blessed *be* God,
Who has not turned away my prayer,
Nor His mercy from me!

Amen.

Cancel All Bad Dreams

The enemies of God cannot move against me without my permission. Not without my permission. I do not consent. I do not give permission. If I have given permission knowingly or unknowingly, I recall that permission, I rescind it, right now, in the Name of Jesus.

I cancel all bad dreams. every demonic dream whether I remember them or not, I bring them all under the Blood of Jesus.

I cancel them all, in the Name of Jesus and in so doing, I cancel any *agreement* with any evil dream, or the devil's plans, in Jesus' Name.

I break all evil agreements made with the demonic, in the Name of Jesus.

Every demon attached to any evil assignment made against me in the spirit realm, I come up against you, in the Name of Jesus.

I declare you must go to the Abyss from where you cannot return, in the Name of Jesus.

Go to the Abyss from where you cannot return in the Name of Jesus. Go! Go!

Anything put in me because of an agreement, I break those evil agreements against me now, in the Name of Jesus.

Only God's will, plans and purposes for me will come to pass in my life, in the Name of Jesus.

Holy Spirit, fill me anew, to overflowing, in the Name of Jesus.

Thank You, Lord, It is done, Lord, thank You for peace concerning these evil dreams, in the Name of Jesus.

I stop every evil dream from manifesting in my life: Anything the Lord has not planted shall be uprooted, in the Name of Jesus.

Feeding in the dream that is setting me up for bewitchment, I rebuke it, in the Name of Jesus. I cancel it.

All *dream defilement*: I bind you from defiling me in the dream and beguiling me in the dream or in the natural, in the Name of Jesus.

Queen of heaven, Astarte, Queen of the coast, Virgin Mary, Mother of rebellion, Mother of harlots, Marine *jezebel spirits* the Lord Jesus rebuke you now. be bound from operating against me, or sending lesser demons under your authority against me, and lesser *spirits* from operating against me, in the Name of Jesus.

Lord, If I am soul tied or covenanted in any way with any evil demon in any way, I break those soul ties now, and serve you a bill of divorce against all evil entities from the dream and in the spirit, in the Name of Jesus.

I declare I am in covenant with the Most High God and Him only. I serve Him, alone, in the Name of Jesus.

All else must leave, you must not torment, or punish me in any way for serving Jehovah, the Most High God, in the Name of Jesus.

Household Witchcraft

Every witch: die by your own machinations; die by your own words, die by your own enchantments, die by your own bewitchments spells, and incantations, back to sender 1000 times, in the Name of Jesus.

Back to sender 1000 times, in the Name of Jesus.

The wrath of God be upon you, in Jesus' Name. Amen.

@ **MIDNIGHT,** Lord, I accuse whosoever has been operating in dark arts and witchcraft against me in the Name of Jesus. I counter accuse every accusers, and I take all of these *whosoevers* to the Courts of Zion at 12 midnight and pray Mercy for myself and ask for judgment of God against all of them, in the Name of Jesus.

Every evil mark, every blade-like mark, every cut, scrape--, I reject it. Every evil in my blood I reject it, in the Name of Jesus. I break the power of all evil marks against me and my life, in the Name of Jesus.

Household witchcraft, stand down (X4).

Household witchcraft stand down, or receive the wrath of God, in the Name of Jesus, (x7).

Remote witchcraft, strange witchcraft, foreign witchcraft, get thee behind me, in the Name of Jesus (x10), or receive the wrath of God now, in the Name of Jesus.

Eating in the dream, sex in dream and any other dream defilement –, I am covered by the Blood of Jesus, in the Blood of Jesus and cannot be defiled. I am in the hand of God and cannot be touched. Touch not God's anointed, do His prophets no harm, in the Name of Jesus. Amen.

Cobwebs to capture my health, strength, wealth, prosperity and joy, or to monitor, I break you by the Fire of the Holy Spirit and command the Thunder of God against the powers that employ you, in the Name of Jesus.

Amen.

Marks of reproach and hatred for no reason, return to sender, in the Name of Jesus.

False accusations, I bind you and return to sender, in the Name of Jesus.

All evil workers of darkness, evil human persecutors, all those that You've arranged deliverance for, Lord, let them be delivered or reserved for such a time that You have ordained for them; let all others receive the Judgement of God now, in the Name of Jesus.

All evil, soulless entities and soulless people, evil human persecutors, die, in the Name of Jesus.

Workers of evil, employees of Satan: drink your own blood and eat your own flesh and die, in the Name of Jesus. (X5)

Psalm 55

Give ear to my prayer, O God; and hide not thyself from my supplication.

Attend unto me, and hear me: I mourn in my complaint, and make a noise;

Because of the voice of the enemy, because of the oppression of the wicked: for they cast iniquity upon me, and in wrath they hate me.

My heart is sore pained within me: and the terrors of death are fallen upon me.

Fearfulness and trembling are come upon me, and horror hath overwhelmed me.

And I said, Oh that I had wings like a dove! for then would I fly away, and be at rest.

Lo, then would I wander far off, and remain in the wilderness. Selah.

I would hasten my escape from the windy storm and tempest.

Destroy, O Lord, and divide their tongues: for I have seen violence and strife in the city.

Day and night they go about it upon the walls thereof: mischief also and sorrow are in the midst of it.

Wickedness is in the midst thereof: deceit and guile depart not from her streets.

For it was not an enemy that reproached me; then I could have borne it: neither was it he that hated me that did magnify himself against me; then I would have hid myself from him:

But it was thou, a man mine equal, my guide, and mine acquaintance.

We took sweet counsel together, and walked unto the house of God in company.

Let death seize upon them, and let them go down quick into hell: for wickedness is in their dwellings, and among them.

As for me, I will call upon God; and the LORD shall save me.

Evening, and morning, and at noon, will I pray, and cry aloud: and he shall hear my voice.

He hath delivered my soul in peace from the battle that was against me: for there were many with me.

God shall hear, and afflict them, even he that abideth of old. Selah. Because they have no changes, therefore they fear not God.

He hath put forth his hands against such as be at peace with him: he hath broken his covenant.

The words of his mouth were smoother than butter, but war was in his heart: his words were softer than oil, yet were they drawn swords.

Cast thy burden upon the LORD, and he shall sustain thee: he shall never suffer the righteous to be moved.

But thou, O God, shalt bring them down into the pit of destruction: bloody and deceitful men shall not live out half their days; but I will trust in thee.

Psalm 58 *(Witches must die, eat your own flesh/drink your own blood and die, in the Name of Jesus. 2 of 3).*

Do ye indeed speak righteousness, O congregation? do ye judge uprightly, O ye sons of men?

Yea, in heart ye work wickedness; ye weigh the violence of your hands in the earth.

The wicked are estranged from the womb: they go astray as soon as they be born, speaking lies.

Their poison is like the poison of a serpent: they are like the deaf adder that stoppeth her ear;

Which will not hearken to the voice of charmers, charming never so wisely.

Break their teeth, O God, in their mouth: break out the great teeth of the young lions, O LORD.

Let them melt away as waters which run continually: when he bendeth his bow to shoot his arrows, let them be as cut in pieces.

As a snail which melteth, let every one of them pass away: like the untimely birth of a woman, that they may not see the sun.

Before your pots can feel the thorns, he shall take them away as with a whirlwind, both living, and in his wrath.

The righteous shall rejoice when he seeth the vengeance: he shall wash his feet in the blood of the wicked.

So that a man shall say, Verily there is a reward for the righteous: verily he is a God that judgeth in the earth.

Psalm 94 (witches die, eat your own flesh/drink your own blood and die, in the Name of Jesus.

Psalm 94 *(3 of 3)*

O Lord God, to whom vengeance belongeth; O God, to whom vengeance belongeth, shew thyself.

Lift up thyself, thou judge of the earth: render a reward to the proud.

LORD, how long shall the wicked, how long shall the wicked triumph?

How long shall they utter and speak hard things? and all the workers of iniquity boast themselves?

They break in pieces thy people, O LORD, and afflict thine heritage.

They slay the widow and the stranger, and murder the fatherless.

Yet they say, The LORD shall not see, neither shall the God of Jacob regard it.

Understand, ye brutish among the people: and ye fools, when will ye be wise?

He that planted the ear, shall he not hear? he that formed the eye, shall he not see?

He that chastiseth the heathen, shall not he correct? he that teacheth man knowledge, shall not he know?

The LORD knoweth the thoughts of man, that they are vanity.

Blessed is the man whom thou chastenest, O LORD, and teachest him out of thy law;

That thou mayest give him rest from the days of adversity, until the pit be digged for the wicked.

For the LORD will not cast off his people, neither will he forsake his inheritance.

But judgment shall return unto righteousness: and all the upright in heart shall follow it.

Who will rise up for me against the evildoers? or who will stand up for me against the workers of iniquity?

Unless the LORD had been my help, my soul had almost dwelt in silence.

When I said, My foot slippeth; thy mercy, O LORD, held me up.

In the multitude of my thoughts within me thy comforts delight my soul.

Shall the throne of iniquity have fellowship with thee, which frameth mischief by a law?

They gather themselves together against the soul of the righteous, and condemn the innocent blood.

But the LORD is my defence; and my God is the rock of my refuge.

And he shall bring upon them their own iniquity, and shall cut them off in their own wickedness; yea, the LORD our God shall cut them off.

The LORD JESUS REBUKE YOU, I blast you into oblivion in the Name of Jesus. (X4)

Shall the prey be taken from the mighty, or the lawful captive delivered? But thus saith the LORD, Even the captives of the mighty shall be taken away, and the prey of the terrible shall be delivered: for I will contend with him that contendeth with thee, and I will save thy children. Isaiah 49:24-26

And I will feed them that oppress thee with their own flesh; and they shall be drunken with their own blood, as with sweet wine: and all flesh shall know that I the LORD am thy Savior and thy Redeemer, the mighty One of Jacob.

Amen

Every Evil Agent

Let every evil agent working against me, eat their own flesh and drink their own blood, and perish, in the Name of Jesus.

Every evil marine kingdom agent assigned or working against me, I cage them with the WORD of GOD:

Enemies of God hear the Word of God, hear the Word of the Lord, hear the blast of His trumpet and go deaf and die in the Name of Jesus.

I John, who also am your brother, and companion in tribulation, and in the kingdom and patience of Jesus Christ, was in the isle that is called Patmos, for the word of God, and for the testimony of Jesus Christ. Revelations 1:9-10

I was in the Spirit on the Lord's day, and heard behind me a great voice, as of a trumpet,

Enemies of God hear the Word of the Lord, hear the blast of His Trumpet, go deaf, and die, in the Name of Jesus.

In every way the kingdom of darkness oppresses or covers me, I rebuke it, I reject it, I renounce it and I turn from it. I turn from demonic entertainment, music, fashion, make up, hair extensions and sex--, illegal sex, in the Name of Jesus.

Lord, help me to not be friends with the world. I'll be in the world, but not of it, in the Name of Jesus.

I serve a bill of divorce to the world and all of its forces. I serve a bill of divorce ABBADON and other principalities ---

Bind up every kind of witchcraft black magic, white magick, green magic, sex magic, earth magick, red magick – earth magic, tree magic--, every kind of magick, in the Name of Jesus.

Satan, you will not control me through sex.

Illicit sex, fornication, adultery, all works of the flesh, I bind you, in the Name of Jesus.

I break every covenant made via sex either in the natural or in the dream/sleep, in the Name of Jesus.

I resist all evil, LORD and bring my body under subjection of the Holy Spirit, in the Name of Jesus.

It is better to marry than to burn; Lord let me live in sexual purity, pleasing to You. LORD, help me keep my body under subjection by the Holy Spirit.

I only have sexual relations with my own, covenanted marriage spouse, in the Name of Jesus.

Soul killers, soul murderers... spiritual wickedness in high places, I bind you, in the Name of Jesus.

Scorners, laughers, mockers, in the dream – witches, warlocks... I bind astral travel and I bind you from attacking me, in the Name of Jesus. I bind *familiar spirits* in or out of the dream, the Lord Jesus rebuke you, in the Name of Jesus.

I bring them to the Courts of Zion for sentencing at midnight. At midnight I declare warfare against every evil agent (Leviticus 20:27 and Exodus 22:18).

@MIDNIGHT I declare WARFARE against any entity, person, evil human persecutor. (Isaiah 49:24-26 and Exodus 14:14-15)

Psalm 2 *(Against Evil Agents 1 of 5)*

Why do the heathen rage, and the people imagine a vain thing?

The kings of the earth set themselves, and the rulers take counsel together, against the LORD, and against his anointed, saying,

Let us break their bands asunder, and cast away their cords from us.

He that sitteth in the heavens shall laugh: the LORD shall have them in derision.

Then shall he speak unto them in his wrath, and vex them in his sore displeasure.

Yet have I set my king upon my holy hill of Zion.

I will declare the decree: the LORD hath said unto me, Thou art my Son; this day have I begotten thee.

Ask of me, and I shall give thee the heathen for thine inheritance, and the uttermost parts of the earth for thy possession.

Thou shalt break them with a rod of iron; thou shalt dash them in pieces like a potter's vessel.

Be wise now therefore, O ye kings: be instructed, ye judges of the earth.

Serve the LORD with fear, and rejoice with trembling.

Kiss the Son, lest he be angry, and ye perish from the way, when his wrath is kindled but a little. Blessed are all they that put their trust in him. Amen.

Psalm 18 *(Against Evil Agents 2 of 5)*

I will love You, O LORD, my strength.
The LORD is my rock and my fortress and my
deliverer;
My God, my strength, in whom I will trust;
My shield and the horn of my salvation, my
stronghold.
I will call upon the LORD, *who is worthy* to be
praised;
So shall I be saved from my enemies.
The pangs of death surrounded me,
And the floods of ungodliness made me afraid.
The sorrows of Sheol surrounded me;
The snares of death confronted me.
In my distress I called upon the LORD,
And cried out to my God;
He heard my voice from His temple,
And my cry came before Him, *even* to His ears.
Then the earth shook and trembled;
The foundations of the hills also quaked and
were shaken,
Because He was angry.
Smoke went up from His nostrils,
And devouring fire from His mouth;
Coals were kindled by it.

He bowed the heavens also, and came down
With darkness under His feet.
And He rode upon a cherub, and flew;
He flew upon the wings of the wind.
He made darkness His secret place;
His canopy around Him *was* dark waters
And thick clouds of the skies.
From the brightness before Him,
His thick clouds passed with hailstones and coals
of fire.
The LORD thundered from heaven,
And the Most High uttered His voice,
Hailstones and coals of fire.
He sent out His arrows and scattered the foe,
Lightnings in abundance, and He vanquished
them.
Then the channels of the sea were seen,
The foundations of the world were uncovered
At Your rebuke, O LORD,
At the blast of the breath of Your nostrils.
He sent from above, He took me;
He drew me out of many waters.
He delivered me from my strong enemy,
From those who hated me,
For they were too strong for me.
They confronted me in the day of my calamity,
But the LORD was my support.

He also brought me out into a broad place;
He delivered me because He delighted in me.
The LORD rewarded me according to my
righteousness;
According to the cleanness of my hands
He has recompensed me.
For I have kept the ways of the LORD,
And have not wickedly departed from my God.
For all His judgments *were* before me,
And I did not put away His statutes from me.
I was also blameless ^jbefore Him,
And I kept myself from my iniquity.
Therefore the LORD has recompensed me
according to my righteousness,
According to the cleanness of my hands in His
sight.
With the merciful You will show Yourself
merciful;
With a blameless man You will show Yourself
blameless;
With the pure You will show Yourself pure;
And with the devious You will show Yourself
shrewd.
For You will save the humble people,
But will bring down haughty looks.
For You will light my lamp;
The LORD my God will enlighten my darkness.

For by You I can run against a troop,
By my God I can leap over a wall.
As for God, His way *is* perfect;
The word of the LORD is proven;
He *is* a shield to all who trust in Him.
For who *is* God, except the LORD?
And who *is* a rock, except our God?
It is God who arms me with strength,
And makes my way perfect.
He makes my feet like the *feet of* deer,
And sets me on my high places.
He teaches my hands to make war,
So that my arms can bend a bow of bronze.
You have also given me the shield of Your
salvation;
Your right hand has held me up,
Your gentleness has made me great.
You enlarged my path under me,
So my feet did not slip.
I have pursued my enemies and overtaken them;
Neither did I turn back again till they were
destroyed.
I have wounded them,
So that they could not rise;
They have fallen under my feet.
For You have armed me with strength for the
battle;

You have subdued under me those who rose up against me.
You have also given me the necks of my enemies,
So that I destroyed those who hated me.
They cried out, but *there was* none to save;
Even to the LORD, but He did not answer them.
Then I beat them as fine as the dust before the wind;
I cast them out like dirt in the streets.
You have delivered me from the strivings of the people;
You have made me the head of the nations;
A people I have not known shall serve me.
As soon as they hear of me they obey me;
The foreigners submit to me.
The foreigners fade away,
And come frightened from their hideouts.
The LORD lives!
Blessed *be* my Rock!
Let the God of my salvation be exalted.
It is God who avenges me,
And subdues the peoples under me;
He delivers me from my enemies.
You also lift me up above those who rise against me;
You have delivered me from the violent man.

Therefore I will give thanks to You, O LORD,
among the Gentiles,
And sing praises to Your name.
Great deliverance He gives to His king,
And shows mercy to His anointed,
To David and his descendants forevermore.

The LORD *is* my light and my salvation;
Whom shall I fear?
The LORD *is* the strength of my life;
Of whom shall I be afraid?
 When the wicked came against me
To eat up my flesh,
My enemies and foes,
They stumbled and fell.
Though an army may encamp against me,
My heart shall not fear;
Though war may rise against me,
In this I *will be* confident.

One *thing* I have desired of the LORD,
That will I seek:
That I may dwell in the house of the LORD
All the days of my life,
To behold the beauty of the LORD,
And to inquire in His temple.
For in the time of trouble
He shall hide me in His pavilion;
In the secret place of His tabernacle
He shall hide me;
He shall set me high upon a rock.

And now my head shall be lifted up above my
enemies all around me;
Therefore I will offer sacrifices of joy in His
tabernacle;
I will sing, yes, I will sing praises to the LORD.
Hear, O LORD, *when* I cry with my voice!
Have mercy also upon me, and answer me.
When You said, "Seek My face,"
My heart said to You, "Your face, LORD, I will
seek."
Do not hide Your face from me;
Do not turn Your servant away in anger;
You have been my help;
Do not leave me nor forsake me,
O God of my salvation.
When my father and my mother forsake me,
Then the LORD will take care of me.
Teach me Your way, O LORD,
And lead me in a smooth path, because of my
enemies.
Do not deliver me to the will of my adversaries;
For false witnesses have risen against me,
And such as breathe out violence.
I would have lost heart, unless I had believed
That I would see the goodness of the LORD
In the land of the living.

Wait on the LORD;
Be of good courage,
And He shall strengthen your heart;
Wait, I say, on the LORD!

Psalm 35

Plead *my cause,* O LORD, with those who strive
with me;
Fight against those who fight against me.
Take hold of shield and buckler,
And stand up for my help.
Also draw out the spear,
And stop those who pursue me.
Say to my soul,
"I *am* your salvation."
Let those be put to shame and brought to
dishonor
Who seek after my life;
Let those be turned back and brought to
confusion
Who plot my hurt.
Let them be like chaff before the wind,
And let the [c]angel of the LORD chase *them.*
Let their way be dark and slippery,
And let the angel of the LORD pursue them.
For without cause they have hidden their net for
me *in* a pit,
Which they have dug without cause for my life.

Let destruction come upon him unexpectedly,
And let his net that he has hidden catch himself;
Into that very destruction let him fall.
And my soul shall be joyful in the LORD;
It shall rejoice in His salvation.
All my bones shall say, "LORD, who *is* like You,
Delivering the poor from him who is too strong
for him,
Yes, the poor and the needy from him who
plunders him?"
Fierce witnesses rise up;
They ask me *things* that I do not know.
They reward me evil for good,
To the sorrow of my soul.
But as for me, when they were sick,
My clothing *was* sackcloth;
I humbled myself with fasting;
And my prayer would return to my own heart.
I paced about as though *he were* my
friend *or* brother;
I bowed down heavily, as one who mourns *for*
his mother.
But in my adversity they rejoiced
And gathered together;
Attackers gathered against me,
And I did not know *it;*
They tore *at me* and did not cease;

With ungodly mockers at feasts
They gnashed at me with their teeth.
Lord, how long will You look on?
Rescue me from their destructions,
My precious *life* from the lions.
I will give You thanks in the great assembly;
I will praise You among many people.
Let them not rejoice over me who are wrongfully
my enemies;
Nor let them wink with the eye who hate me
without a cause.
For they do not speak peace,
But they devise deceitful matters
Against *the* quiet ones in the land.
They also opened their mouth wide against me,
And said, "Aha, aha!
Our eyes have seen *it.*"
This You have seen, O LORD;
Do not keep silence.
O Lord, do not be far from me.
Stir up Yourself, and awake to my vindication,
To my cause, my God and my Lord.
Vindicate me, O LORD my God, according to
Your righteousness;
And let them not rejoice over me.
Let them not say in their hearts, "Ah, so we

would have it!"
Let them not say, "We have swallowed him up."
Let them be ashamed and brought to mutual
confusion
Who rejoice at my hurt;
Let them be clothed with shame and dishonor
Who exalt themselves against me.
Let them shout for joy and be glad,
Who favor my righteous cause;
And let them say continually,
"Let the LORD be magnified,
Who has pleasure in the prosperity of His
servant."
And my tongue shall speak of Your
righteousness
And of Your praise all day long.

Psalm 109 Plea for Judgment of False Accusers
(Against Evil Agents 5 of 5)

Do not keep silent, O God of my praise!
For the mouth of the wicked and the mouth of the deceitful
Have opened against me;
They have spoken against me with a lying tongue.
They have also surrounded me with words of hatred,
And fought against me without a cause.
In return for my love they are my accusers,
But I *give myself to* prayer.
Thus they have rewarded me evil for good,
And hatred for my love.
Set a wicked man over him,
And let an accuser stand at his right hand.
When he is judged, let him be found guilty,
And let his prayer become sin.
Let his days be few, *And* let another take his office.
Let his children be fatherless, And his wife a widow.
Let his children continually be vagabonds, and beg;

Let them seek *their bread* also from their desolate places.
Let the creditor seize all that he has,
And let strangers plunder his labor.
Let there be none to extend mercy to him,
Nor let there be any to favor his fatherless children.
Let his posterity be cut off,
And in the generation following let their name be blotted out.
Let the iniquity of his fathers be remembered before the LORD,
And let not the sin of his mother be blotted out.
Let them be continually before the LORD,
That He may cut off the memory of them from the earth;
Because he did not remember to show mercy,
But persecuted the poor and needy man,
That he might even slay the broken in heart.
As he loved cursing, so let it come to him;
As he did not delight in blessing, so let it be far from him.
As he clothed himself with cursing as with his garment,
So let it enter his body like water,
And like oil into his bones.
Let it be to him like the garment which covers

him,
And for a belt with which he girds himself
continually.
Let this *be* the LORD's reward to my accusers,
And to those who speak evil against my person.
But You, O GOD the Lord,
Deal with me for Your name's sake;
Because Your mercy *is* good, deliver me.
For I *am* poor and needy,
And my heart is wounded within me.
I am gone like a shadow when it lengthens;
I am shaken off like a locust.
My knees are weak through fasting,
And my flesh is feeble from lack of fatness.
I also have become a reproach to them;
When they look at me, they shake their heads.
Help me, O LORD my God!
Oh, save me according to Your mercy,
That they may know that this *is* Your hand—
That You, LORD, have done it!
Let them curse, but You bless;
When they arise, let them be ashamed,
But let Your servant rejoice.
Let my accusers be clothed with shame,
And let them cover themselves with their own
disgrace as with a mantle.

I will greatly praise the LORD with my mouth;
Yes, I will praise Him among the multitude.
For He shall stand at the right hand of the poor,
To save *him* from those who condemn him.
Amen.

Lord, thank You for warning that witches are plotting against me. Thank You for the warnings that come in the dream: Sex in the dream, eating in the dream, haircut in the dream, hair braided in the dream, cow butchered in the dream, at the market in the dream, wild birds eating flesh in the dream. Wild beast or cats in the dream. Constant nightmares--

Thank You for the warnings that I may bring them to the Throne for judgment, in the Name of Jesus.

Where Is My Money?

Lord, where is my money?

Crooked thieves, enemies of GOD and enemies of mine I forbid you to divert my money, now, or ever again, in the future. And I proclaim that everything you've stolen from me must be returned 7 fold, in the Name of Jesus.

Thank You for showing me in the dream. Every time I see myself I beggarly clothes, let it backfire and be canceled out of my life, in the Name of Jesus.

LORD, thank You that You show me their plans and tactics of the devil, in the dream, in the Name of Jesus.

Lord, I receive increase at Your hand, in the Name of Jesus.

For promotion cometh neither from the east, nor from the west, Nor from the south. But – from You; You are the Judge. Promotion comes from You.

He putteth down one, and setteth up another. Promotion comes from the Lord, Amen. (Psalm 75:6-7)

Every good gift and every perfect gift is from above, and cometh down from the Father of lights, with whom is no variableness, neither shadow of turning. Amen. (James 1:17)

Blessings of God locate me now, in the Name of Jesus.

I open wide all doors leading to my blessings, victory and breakthroughs which the enemies have closed, in the Name of Jesus.

Hunters after my soul, my flesh, my blood, have they no knowledge, all the evildoers who eat up my people as they eat bread and do not call upon the LORD? NIV

Do not all these evildoers know nothing? They devour My people, says the Lord, as though eating bread; they never call on the Lord.

And call upon me in the day of trouble: I will deliver thee, and thou shalt glorify Me, says the Lord. Amen.

Now tell them this: 'As surely as I live, declares the LORD, I will do to you the very things I heard you say. (Numbers 14:28 NLT)

Thank You Lord, I am a *speaking Spirit* and I can declare with my own voice and give voice to the Words of the Lord God. And He shall hear and do as I say, in the Name of Jesus. Thank You, Lord.

Stir me up, wake me up, get me up to pray, Holy Spirit and let me pray let me pray, teach me to pray properly, when any is coming after my destiny, my life, my prosperity, my marriage, my relationship with God, in the Name of Jesus.

I call on You, Father, to contend with those that contend with me. I **must** speak because if I don't, You will think I agree with my enemies who are against me; I do not agree with them, I do not form alliance with them, I do not accept this treatment. I do not accept it.

Lord, every battle I have not seen, I come against it, in the Name of Jesus.

Every battle I have inherited, I come against it, in the Name of Jesus.

Every battle that I have ignored; thank You Lord for showing me. I come against it, in the Name of Jesus.

Every battle I have not known what to do, Holy Spirit, teach me. Thank You for teaching me what to do, and the power of God helping me to do it, in the Name of Jesus.

Every power after my finances and after me to make me suffer. I bind you and I come after you, in the Name of Jesus.

Every witchcraft trap, be caught in your own trap, be caught in your own net, be caught in your own snare. Every fowler's snare, every trap set in plain sight, in front of me, Lord do not let me fall into it. Do not let me fall into pits, traps, nets and snares, in the Name of Jesus.

Every *monitoring spirit* looking for an unguarded hour against me--, Angels of God, guardian angels watch over me, day and night so there are no unguarded hours in the day or in the night, in the Name of Jesus.

Lord, @MIDNIGHT the third watch of the evening, I declare this Warfare.

Every evil must bow at the Name of Jesus Christ.

I use the spiritual weapons of warfare, the Name of the LORD, the Blood of the Lamb, the Word of God, keys of the Kingdom of Heaven—binding and loosing, the Razor of the Lord, all tokens of the LORD. LORD open Your armory and let me get and use the weapons that I am authorized to use against the enemies of my life, of my soul, of my spirit and my relationship with You, in the Name of Jesus.

Every power bent on destroying me, destroying mankind bow to the Name of Jesus. **JESUS, JESUS, JESUS. Jesus Christ**. You must bow to the Name of Jesus Christ.

Spirits of fornication, lust, adultery, greed, materialism, disobedience, rebellion and grieving the Holy Spirit. I bind and cast you out, in the Name of Jesus.

If someone throws an evil arrow at me – thank You Lord, thank You Lord--, do not let there be anything in me to cause that arrow to land or strike me. Lord, I bind up all works of the flesh and all evil, all wickedness in myself and I cast it out. I command it to leave, Leave my life! And I resist the devil and he must leave, in the Name of Jesus.

Lord, don't let me be a liar. Do not let the words of my mouth allow demonic access to my body, soul, or spirit, in the Name of Jesus.

Lord, let the words of my mouth and the meditation of my heart be acceptable to You, in the Name of Jesus. Amen.

Lord, help me to keep my environment appropriate for the blessings of the Lord to come upon me. Thank You, Lord, let your Holy Spirit change me. Let me submit and yield and move me so I can be more like You, in the Name of Jesus.

Lord, everything the Holy Spirit is telling me to move and change, take away from my environment, the clothes I wear, music I own, CD's DVD's, movies, demonic books, jewelry, and everything demonic – even décor – it must go, in the Name of Jesus. So that I live by the truth of the Word of God.

Enemies of GOD, entities after me --- I cage you by the Word of God, by the ordinances of GOD, - and I lock you in spiritual prison for millennia, in the Name of Jesus.

Psalm 91 *(Where Is My Money 1 of 1)*

He that dwelleth in the secret place of the most
High shall abide under the shadow of the
Almighty.

I will say of the LORD, He is my refuge and my
fortress: my God; in him will I trust.

Surely he shall deliver thee from the snare of the
fowler, and from the noisome pestilence.

He shall cover thee with his feathers, and under his
wings shalt thou trust: his truth shall be thy shield
and buckler.

Thou shalt not be afraid for the terror by night; nor
for the arrow that flieth by day;

Nor for the pestilence that walks at darkness; nor
for the destruction that wasteth at noonday.

A thousand shall fall at thy side, and ten thousand
at thy right hand; but it shall not come nigh thee,
(says the Lord).

Only with thine eyes shalt thou behold and see the
reward of the wicked.

Because thou hast made the LORD, which is my refuge, even the most High, thy habitation;

There shall no evil befall thee, neither shall any plague come nigh thy dwelling.

For he shall give his angels charge over thee, to keep thee in all thy ways.

They shall bear thee up in their hands, lest thou dash thy foot against a stone.

Thou shalt tread upon the lion and adder: the young lion and the dragon shalt thou trample under feet.

Because he hath set his love upon me, therefore will I deliver him: I will set him on high, because he hath known my name.

He shall call upon me, and I will answer him: I will be with him in trouble; I will deliver him and honour him.

With long life will I satisfy him and shew him my salvation. AMEN.

For the Son of man is come to seek and to save that which was lost. (Luke 19:10)

Lord, if I am none of yours, make me one of yours in the Name of Jesus.

And they overcame him by the blood of the Lamb, and by the word of their testimony; and they loved not their lives unto the death, (Revelation 12:11).

Lord, forgive me for reckless words in the Name of Jesus. The Words I speak; they are Spirit and they are life, let them be acceptable to you, in the Name of Jesus. (John 6:63)

Lord, forgive me for reckless thoughts because they are spirit, in the Name of Jesus.

Thak You, Lord, it is illegal to have anything happen to me in this earth that I have not agreed to. I rescind all permissions from all workers of iniquity, all workers of evil and the devil himself in the Name of Jesus.

"I declare that I am freeborn of God. By virtue of my spiritual birthright as a child of God, I decide what to allow or what not to allow in my life. Therefore every evil projected or programmed against me that is coming against me from any direction--, I reject you now in Jesus' Name." (X4)

Extract Myself from Satan

@ MIDNIGHT, Lord, I have come with this warfare.

> And he said unto them, I beheld Satan as lightning fall from heaven. Behold, I give unto you power to tread on serpents and scorpions, and over all the power of the enemy: and nothing shall by any means hurt you. (Luke 10:18-19).

@MIDNIGHT Lord, while Satan is busy, I extract myself from him, from his captivity, from his jails, prisons and cells, I extract by the power in the Blood of Jesus, by help of the mighty Warrior Angels of God. I am extracted. I extract myself, my possessions, my glory, my health, my strength, my prosperity, my purpose, my destiny, life, my career, my education, my dignity, my honor, my marriage, my family, my children, my worship, my wisdom, my knowledge—mind, intellect, my faculties, my Godly imagination and creativity --, everything that belongs to my peace, I extract it back from the devil and from the strongmen guarding every strongroom, and from all those who work for the devil, in the Name of Jesus.

LORD, rescue me, do not leave my soul in hell.

Restore to me all that has been lost, stolen, and even destroyed so that I will have and enjoy the abundant life that Jesus came and died on Calvary for me to have in this life and in the life to come, in the Name of Jesus, Amen.

Thus shall ye say unto them, The *gods* that have not made the heavens and the earth, even they shall perish from the earth, and from under these heavens, in the Name of Jesus. (Jeremiah 10:11 (X3))

Thank You, Lord. Thank You, Lord.

Psalm 92 *(Extract Myself from Satan 1 of 1)*

It is a good thing to give thanks unto the LORD, and to sing praises unto thy name, O Most High:

To shew forth thy lovingkindness in the morning, and thy faithfulness every night,

Upon an instrument of ten strings, and upon the psaltery; upon the harp with a solemn sound.

For thou, LORD, hast made me glad through thy work: I will triumph in the works of thy hands.

O LORD, how great are thy works! and thy thoughts are very deep.

A brutish man knoweth not; neither doth a fool understand this.

When the wicked spring as the grass, and when all the workers of iniquity do flourish; it is that they shall be destroyed forever:

But thou, LORD, art most high for evermore.

For, lo, thine enemies, O LORD, for, lo, thine enemies shall perish; all the workers of iniquity shall be scattered.

But my horn shalt thou exalt like the horn of an unicorn: I shall be anointed with fresh oil.

Mine eye also shall see my desire on mine enemies, and mine ears shall hear my desire of the wicked that rise up against me.

The righteous shall flourish like the palm tree: he shall grow like a cedar in Lebanon.

Those that be planted in the house of the LORD shall flourish in the courts of our God.

They shall still bring forth fruit in old age; they shall be fat and flourishing;

To shew that the LORD is upright: he is my rock, and there is no unrighteousness in him.

Vengeance Belongs to God

God of Vengeance, show Yourself strong and mighty, in the Name of Jesus.

Righteous Judge of the entire universe You rule in righteousness. Judge against the enemies of my soul, in Jesus' Name. Do not let the wicked continue to triumph over my soul, in Jesus' Name.

Lord, shut the mouth of the wicked against me, forever, in the Name of Jesus.

Lord, bind up their enchantments, incantations, curses, and spells, in the Name of Jesus Lord, give me rest from all this adversary and all this adversity, let me dwell in safety, let me sleep and have rest and receive all things that pertain to my peace, in the Name of Jesus.

I shall live and not die but declare the works of the Lord, in the land of the living, in the Name of Jesus.

Lord, I know you will never leave me or forsake me, and that vengeance is Yours, Lord. Judgment is Yours. Vengeance is not mine, neither does it belong to witches or to Satan. Vengeance is the Lord's.

Lord, rise up for me against all evil doers, in the Name of Jesus. Lord You are my help, else I would have suffered alone and in silence.

Lord, You held me up when my foot slipped, thank You, Lord.

Lord, judge all those that gather together against the righteous to condemn innocent blood and without cause, or without just cause, in the Name of Jesus.

You, Lord, are my defense, the Rock of my refuge. You are the Rock of Ages.

Lord, You shall bring upon them their own iniquity, and shall cut them off in their own wickedness; yea, the LORD our God shall cut them off.

Amen.

Psalm 108 *(Vengeance Belongs to God, 1 of 1)*

O God, my heart is fixed; I will sing and give praise, even with my glory.

Awake, psaltery and harp: I myself will awake early.

I will praise thee, O LORD, among the people: and I will sing praises unto thee among the nations.

For thy mercy is great above the heavens: and thy truth reaches unto the clouds.

Be thou exalted, O God, above the heavens: and thy glory above all the earth;

That thy beloved may be delivered: save with thy right hand, and answer me.

God hath spoken in his holiness; I will rejoice, I will divide Shechem, and mete out the valley of Succoth.

Gilead is mine; Manasseh is mine; Ephraim also is the strength of mine head; Judah is my lawgiver;

Moab is my washpot; over Edom will I cast out my shoe; over Philistia will I triumph.

Who will bring me into the strong city? who will lead me into Edom?

Wilt not thou, O God, who hast cast us off? and wilt not thou, O God, go forth with our hosts?

Give us help from trouble: for vain is the help of man.

Through God we shall do valiantly: for he it is that shall tread down our enemies, (X4), in the Name of Jesus, Amen.

Lord, I bind up retaliation. I enjoin the enemy from using, misusing, twisting and/or perverting the words of this prayer, in the Name of Jesus.

Enemies of God, the Blood of Jesus is between me and you, in the Name of Jesus.

I seal the declarations and decrees of this prayer with the Fire of the Holy Ghost and with the Blood of Jesus across every realm, age, timeline and dimension, past present and future, to infinity, in the Name of Jesus.

AMEN! *Worship the Lord!*

Dear Reader: Thank you for purchasing and reading this book. May God always make you aware of trouble in time to prevent it from touching your life and the lives of your loved ones.

Amen

Dr. Marlene Miles

*This book was inspired by **Masters of Dream Interpretation** by Eugene Godman.*

Prayer against Pleiades, etc taken from a longer prayer by Dr. Daniel Duvall.

Art design adapted from Dreamstime.com

Prayer books by this author

While most books by this author have prayer points either throughout the book or at the end, there are some books that are **only** prayers. You just open up the book and pray. They are listed below:

Prayers Against Barrenness: *For Success in Business and Life*

Fruit of the Womb: *Prayers Against Barrenness*

Beauty Curses, *Warfare Prayers Against*
https://a.co/d/5Xlc20M

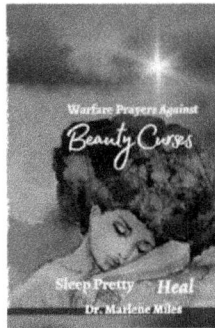

Courts of Marriage: Prayers for Marriage in the Courts of Heaven *(prayerbook)* https://a.co/d/cNAdgAq

Courtroom Warfare @ Midnight *(prayerbook)*
https://a.co/d/5fc7Qdp

Demonic Cobwebs *(prayerbook)* https://a.co/d/fp9Oa2H

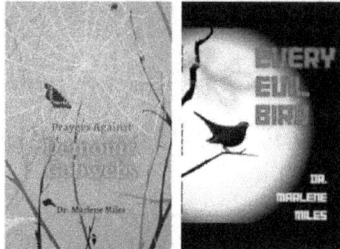

Every Evil Bird https://a.co/d/hF1kh1O

Every Evil Arrow https://a.co/d/afgRkiA

Gates of Thanksgiving

Spirits of Death & the Grave, Pass Over Me and My House https://a.co/d/dS4ewyr

Please note that my name is spelled incorrectly on amazon, but not on the book.

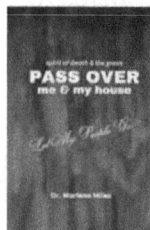

Throne of Grace: Courtroom Prayer

https://a.co/d/fNMxcM9

Warfare Prayer Against Poverty
https://a.co/d/bZ61lYu

Other books by this author

Abundance of Jesus, *The*

AK: *The Adventures of the Agape Kid*

AMONG SOME THIEVES

Ancestral Powers https://a.co/d/9prTyFf

Backstabbers https://a.co/d/gi8iBxf

Barrenness, *Prayers Against*
https://a.co/d/feUltIs

Battlefield of Marriage, *The*

Beware of the Dog: *Prayers Against Dogs in the Dream*

Blindsided: *Has the Old Man Bewitched You?*
https://a.co/d/5O2fLLR

Break Free from Collective Captivity

Caged Life https://a.co/d/0eKxbU9H

Casting Down Imaginations https://a.co/d/1UxlLqa

Churchcraft: Witchcraft In the Church

Churchzilla, The Wanna-Be, Supposed-to-be Bride of Christ

Curses of Blind Men

Demonic Cobwebs (prayerbook)

Demonic Time Bombs

Demons Hate Questions (mini book)

Devil Loves Trauma, *The*

Devil Weapons: Unforgiveness, Bitterness,…

The Devourers: *Thieves of Darkness 2*

Do Not Swear by the Moon

Don't Refuse Me, Lord (4 book series)

https://a.co/d/idP34LG

Dream Defilement

The Emptiers: *Thieves of Darkness, 1*
https://a.co/d/5I4n5mc

Every Evil Arrow https://a.co/d/afgRkiA

Evil Touch https://a.co/d/gSGGpS1

Failed Assignment https://a.co/d/3CXtjZY

Fantasy Spirit Spouse https://a.co/d/hW7oYbX

FAT Demons (The): *Breaking Demonic Curses*

The Fold (5-book series)

- The Fold (Book 1)
- Name Your Seed (Book 2)
- The Poor Attitudes of Money (3)
- Do Not Orphan Your Seed (4)
- For the Sake of the Gospel (5)
- My Sowing Journal

Gang Ups: *Touch Not God's Anointed*

got HEALING? Verses for Life

got LOVE? Verses for Life

got HOPE? Verses for Life

got money? https://a.co/d/g2av41N

Has My Soul Been Sold?

How to Dental Assist

How to Dental Assist2: Be Productive, Not Wasteful

I Take It Back

Legacy

Let Me Have A Dollar's Worth
https://a.co/d/h8F8XgE

Level the Playing Field
https://www.youtube.com/watch?v=BfF-TX1EWNQ

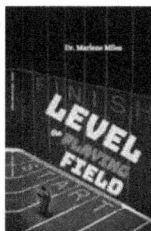

Living for the NOW of God

Lose My Location https://a.co/d/crD6mV9

Love Breaks Your Heart

Man Safari, *The* (mini book from The Wilderness Romance)

Marriage Ed. Rules of Engagement & Marriage

Made Perfect in Love

Money Hunters: Beware of Those

Money on the Altar https://a.co/d/4EqJ2Nr

Mulberry Tree https://a.co/d/9nR9rRb

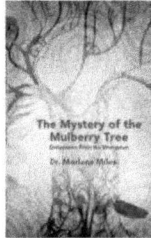

Motherboard (The) - *Soul Prosperity Series*

Name Your Seed

Occupy: *Until I Return*

Plantation Souls

Players Gonna Play

Power Money: Nine Times the Tithe
https://a.co/d/gRt41gy

Powers Above

Repent of Visiting Evil Altars
https://a.co/d/3n3Zjwx

The Robe, *Part 1, The Lessons of Joseph*

The Robe, *The Lessons of Joseph* Part II,

Seasons of Grief

Seasons of Waiting

Seasons of War

Second Marriage, Third--, *Any Marriage*
https://a.co/d/6m6GN4N

Sift You Like Wheat

Six Men Short: What Has Happened to all the Men?

Son https://a.co/d/09mIThSg

Soul Prosperity, Soul Prosperity Series Bk 3
https://a.co/d/5p8YvCN

Souls Captivity, Soul Prosperity Series Book 2

The Spirit of Poverty

StarStruck

SUNBLOCK

The Swallowers: *Thieves of Darkness*, Book 3

Take It Back

This Is NOT That: How to Keep Demons from Coming at You

Time Is of the Essence

Too Many Wives: *Why You Have Lady Problems*

Tormenting Spirits   https://a.co/d/dAogEJf

Toxic Souls

Triangular Power *(series)*

- Powers Above
- SUNBLOCK
- Do Not Swear by the Moon
- STARSTRUCK

Unbreak My Heart: *Don't Let Me Die*
Uncontested Doom

Unguarded Hours, *The*

Unseen Life, *The* https://a.co/d/0drZ5Ll

Upgrade: How to Get Out of Survival Mode
(and two more titles):

- Toxic Souls (Book 2 of series)
- Legacy (Book 3 of series)

WTH? Get Me Out of This Hell

The Wasters: *Thieves of Darkness,* Bk 2
https://a.co/d/bUvI9Jo

What Have You to Declare? What Do You Have
With You from Where You've Been?

When I Was A Child, *I Prayed As a Child*

When the Devourer is Rebuked

https://a.co/d/1HVv8oq

The Wilderness Romance *(series)* This series is about conducting a Godly relationship and marriage with someone who is a Wilderness person. It is about how to recognize it and navigate through it. These books are about how not to get caught up in such.

- *The Social Wilderness*
- *The Sexual Wilderness*
- *The Spiritual Wilderness*

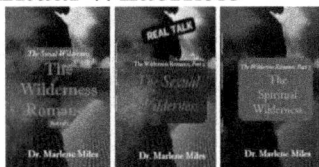

Other Series
Matters of the Heart series

Made Perfect in Love https://a.co/d/7OMQW3O

Love Breaks Your Heart https://a.co/d/4KvuQLZ

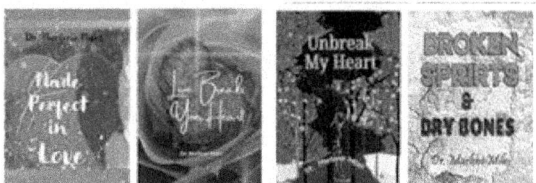

Unbreak My Heart https://a.co/d/84ceZ6M

Broken Spirits & Dry Bones https://a.co/d/e6iedNP

The Fold (a series on Godly finances)

https://a.co/d/4hz3unj

Soul Prosperity Series https://a.co/d/bz2M42q

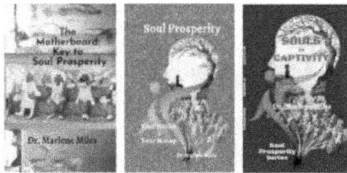

Spirit Spouse books

https://a.co/d/9VehDSo

https://a.co/d/97sKOwm

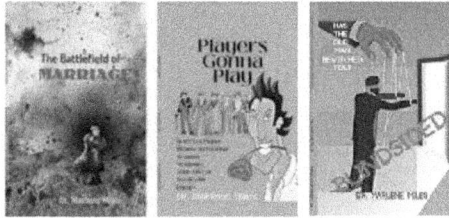

Thieves of Darkness series

https://a.co/d/b07c8Ms

Triangular Powers https://a.co/d/aUCjAWC

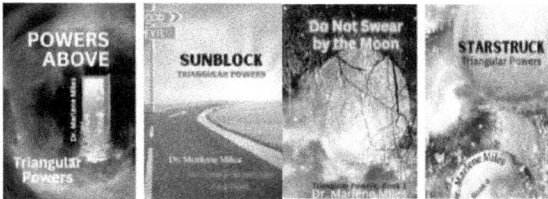

Upgrade (series) *How to Get Out of Survival Mode*
https://a.co/d/aTERhXO

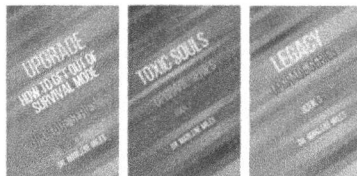

www.ingramcontent.com/pod-product-compliance
Lightning Source LLC
Chambersburg PA
CBHW061831040426
42447CB00012B/2915